TRIPPIN' SNEAKS

Far Out Sneakers Coloring Book

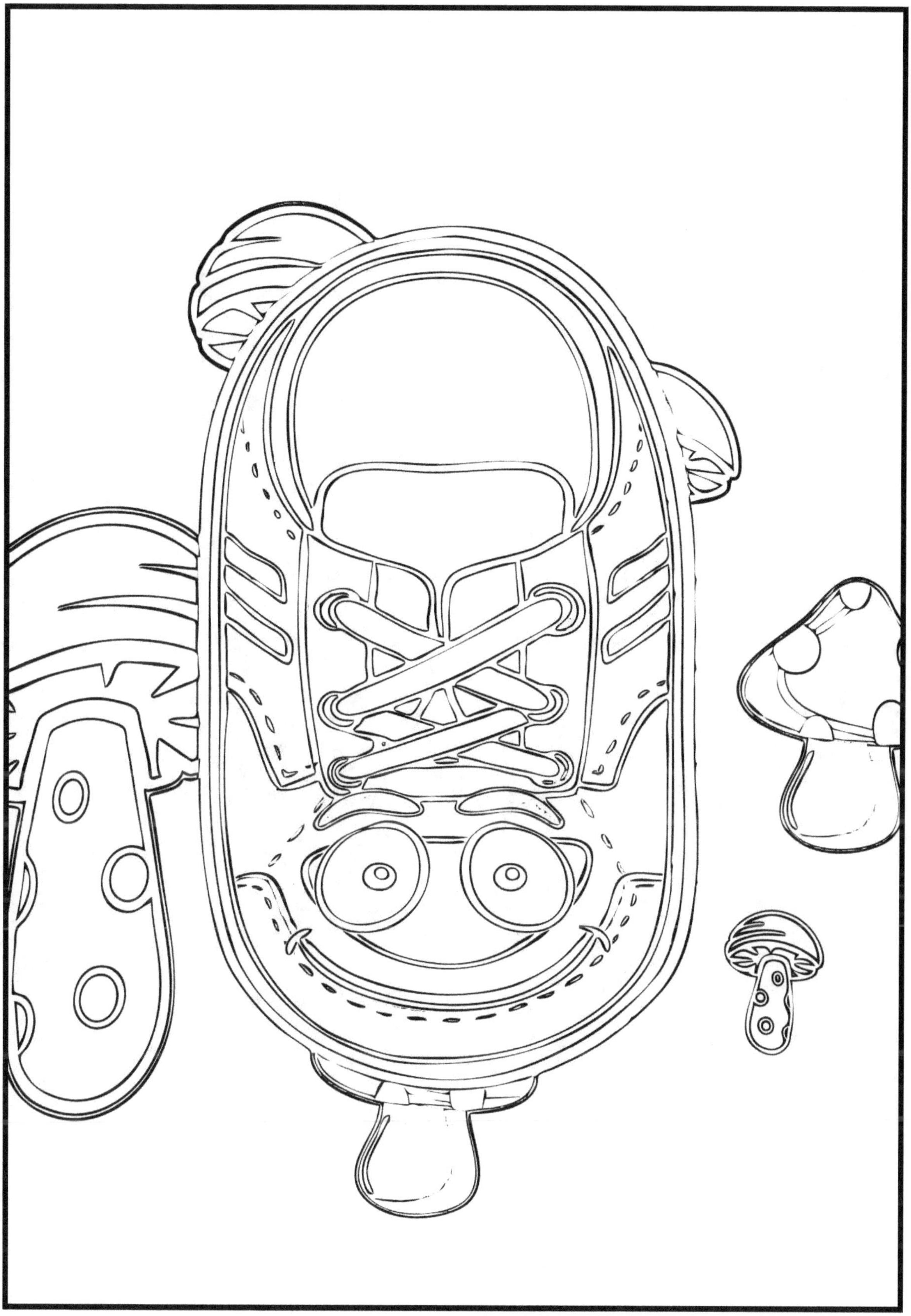

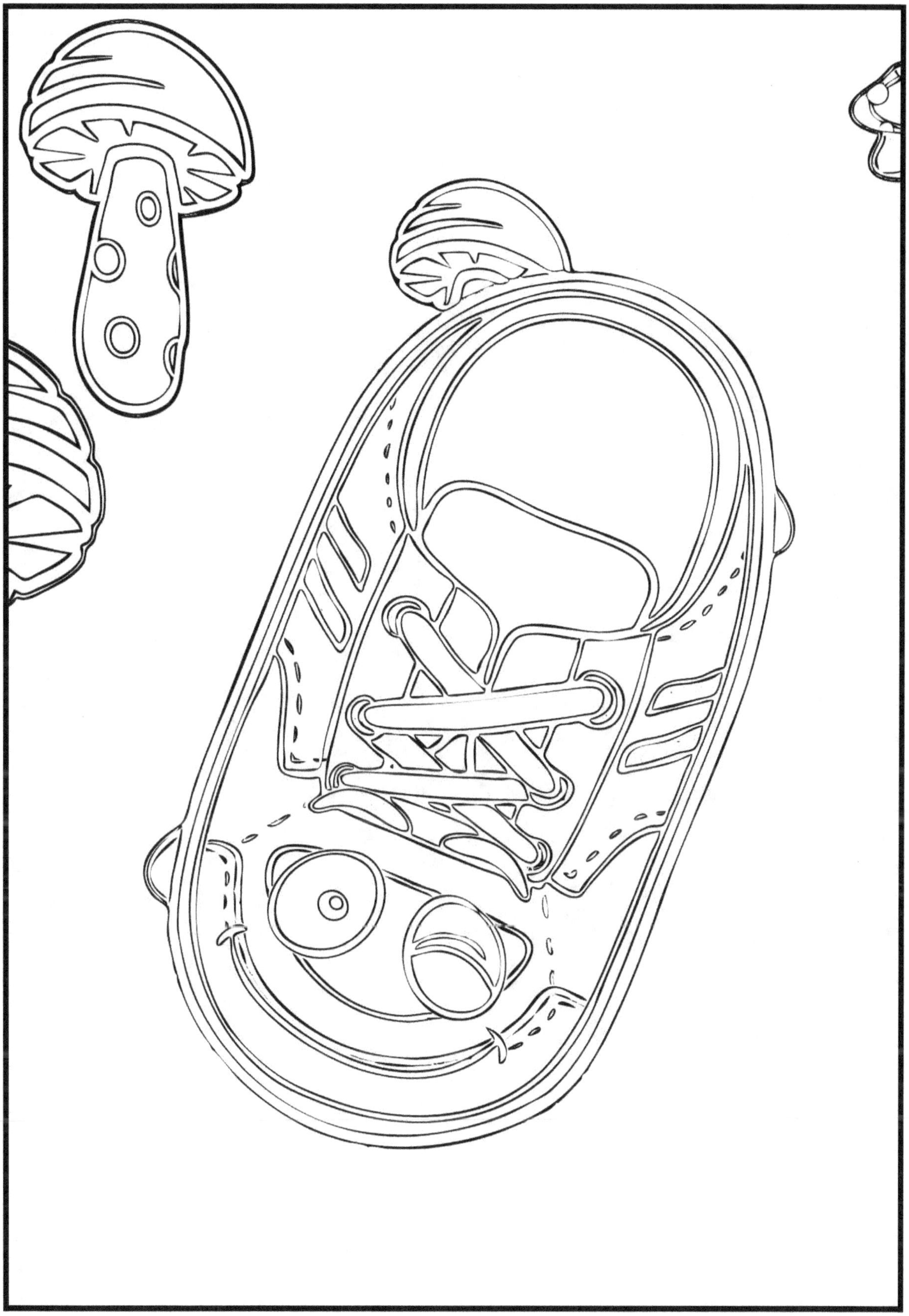

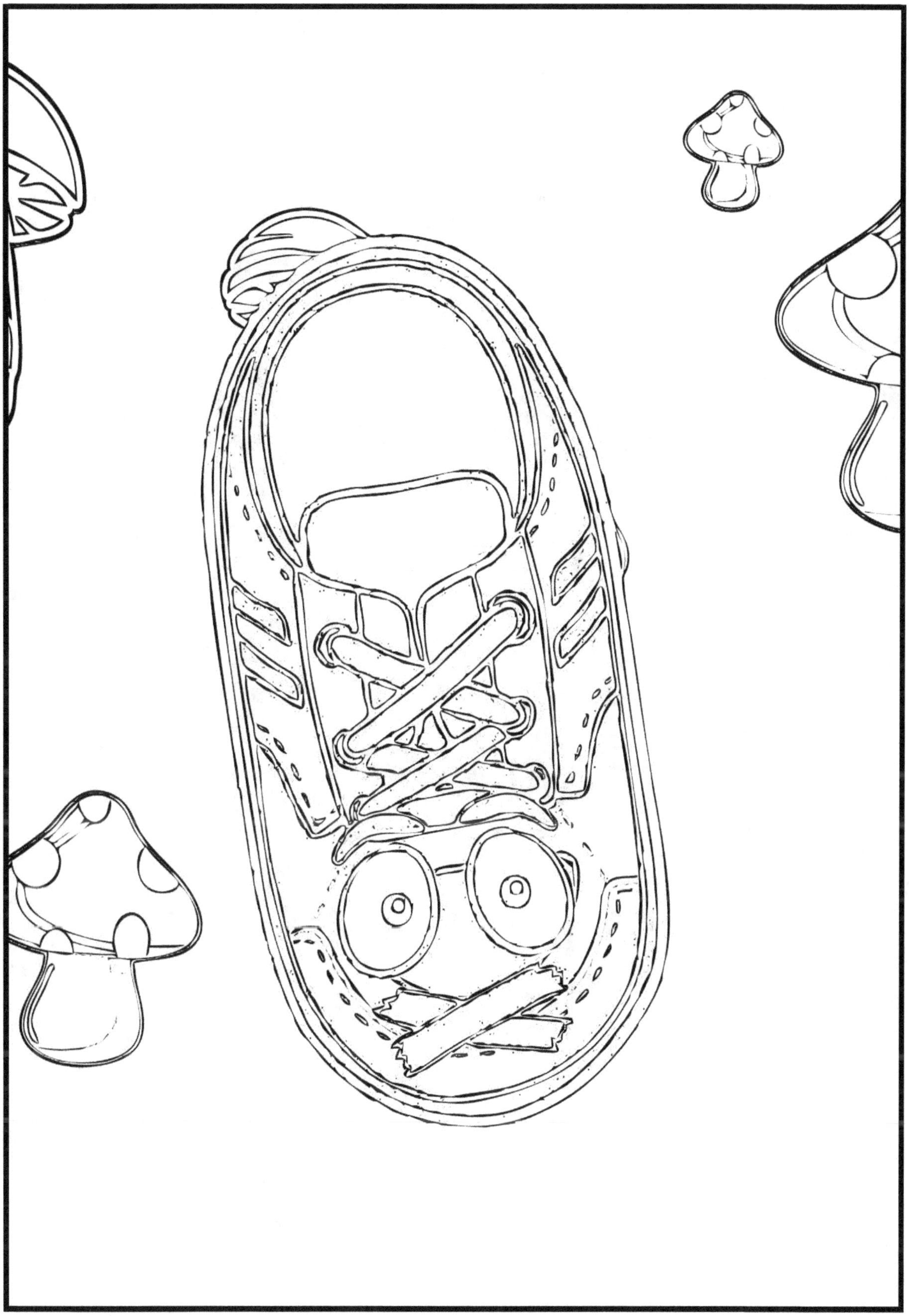

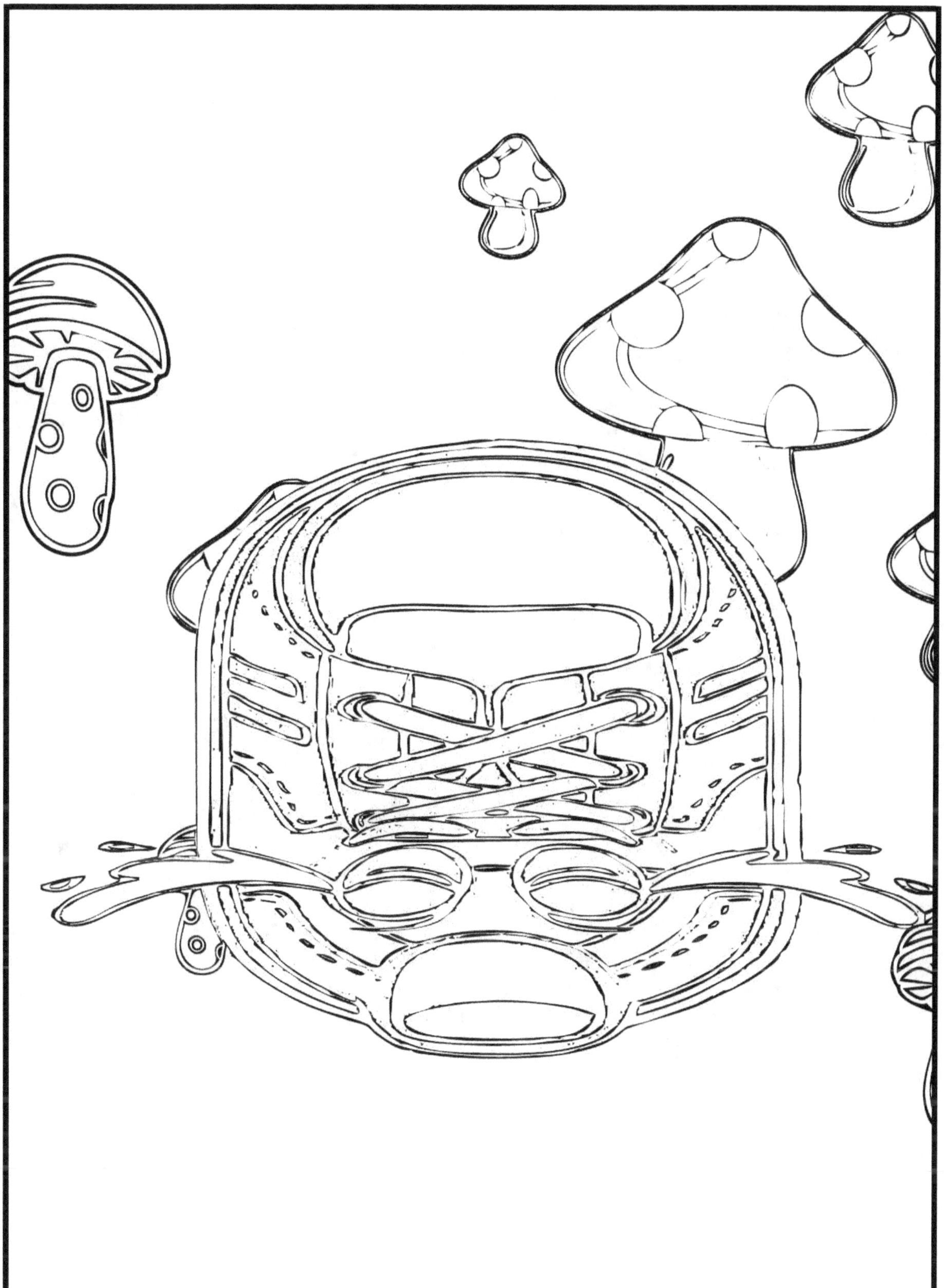

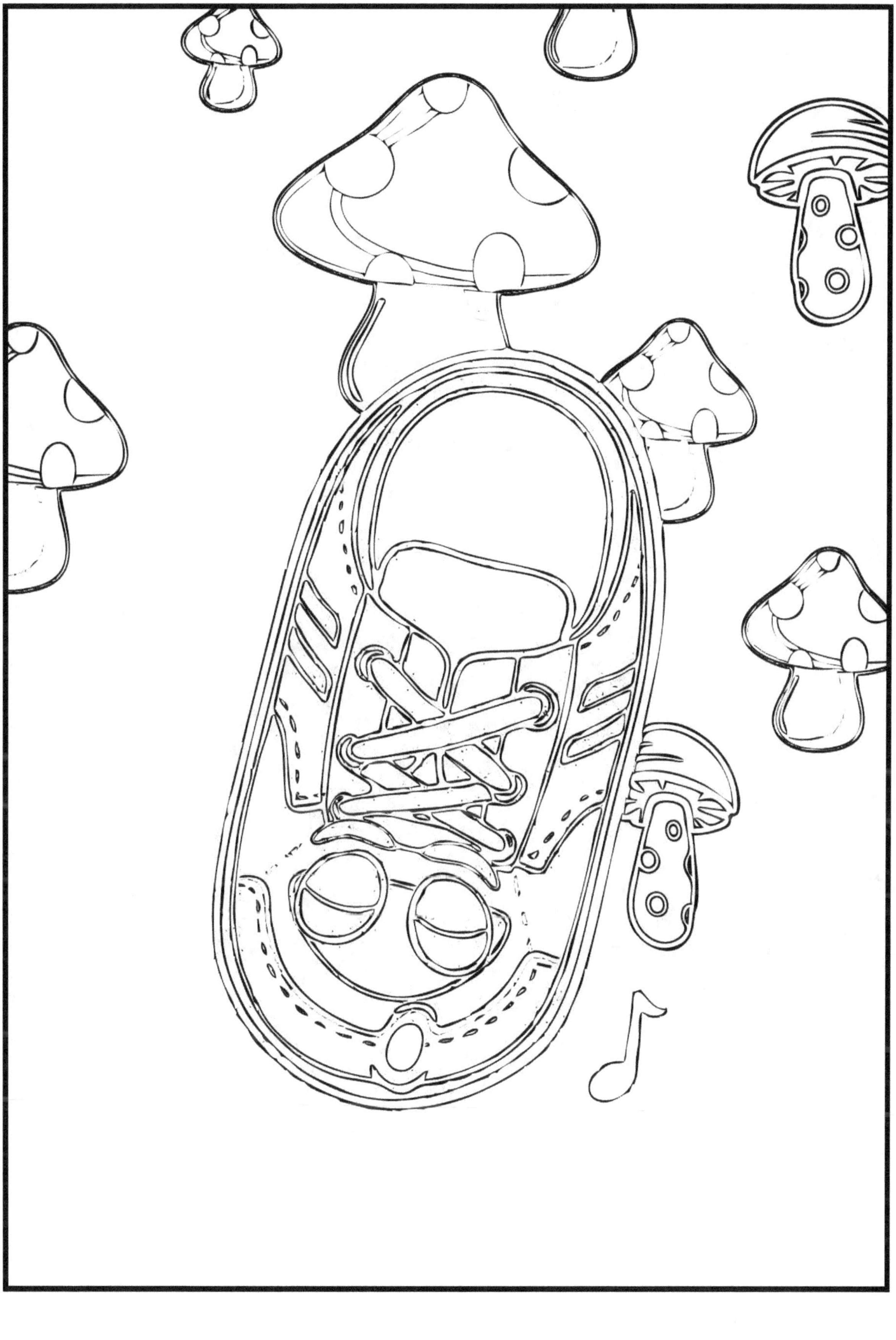

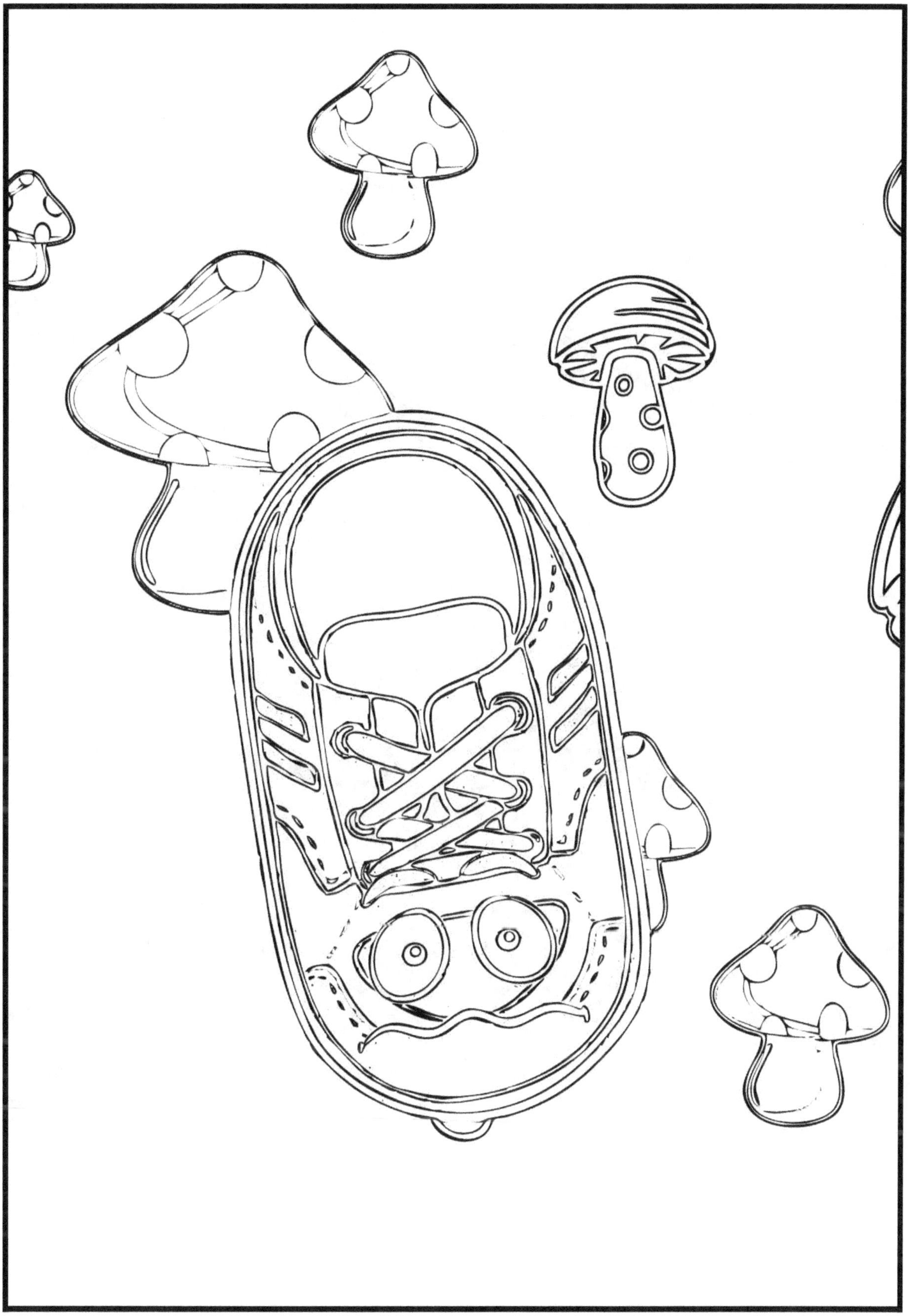

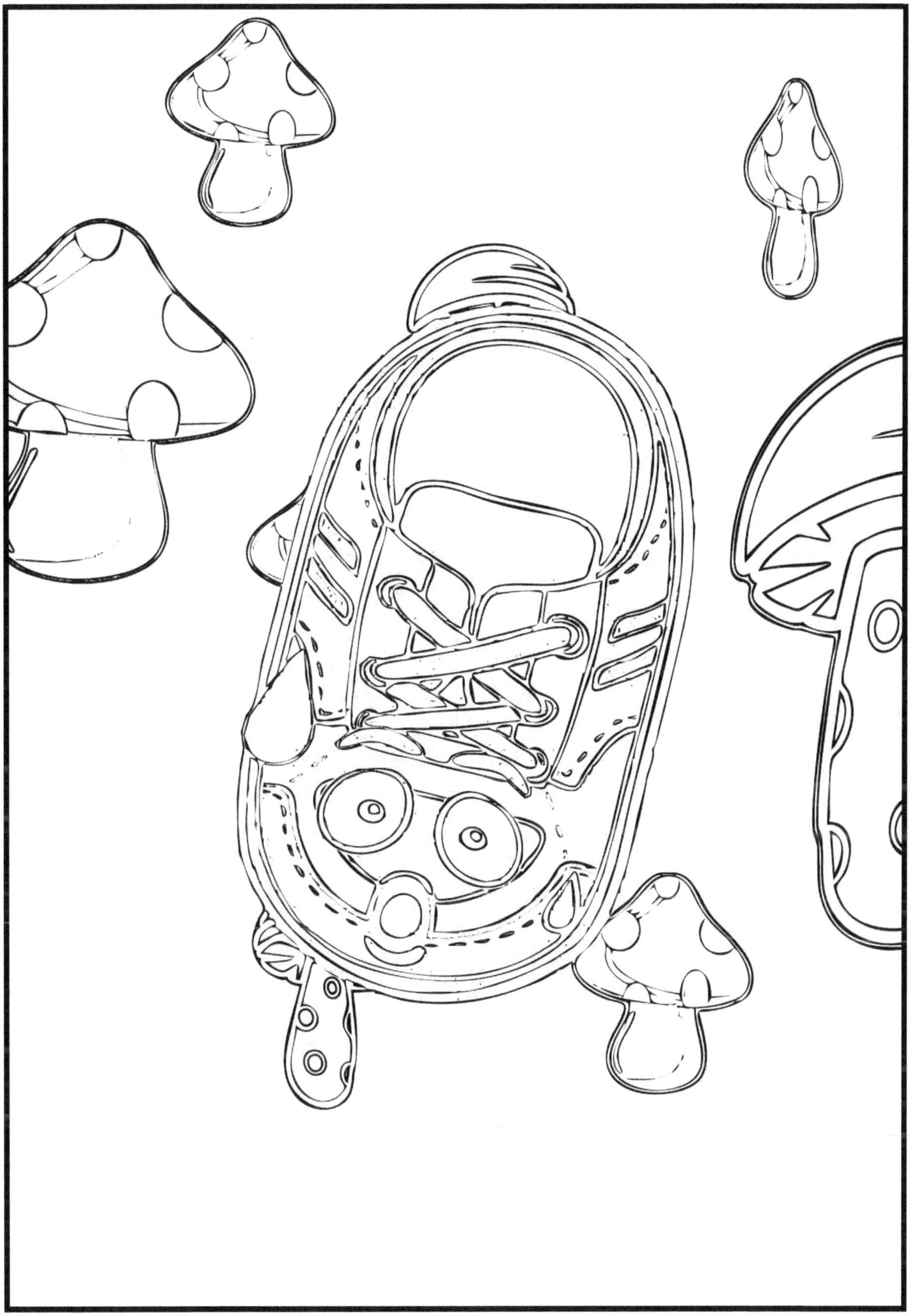

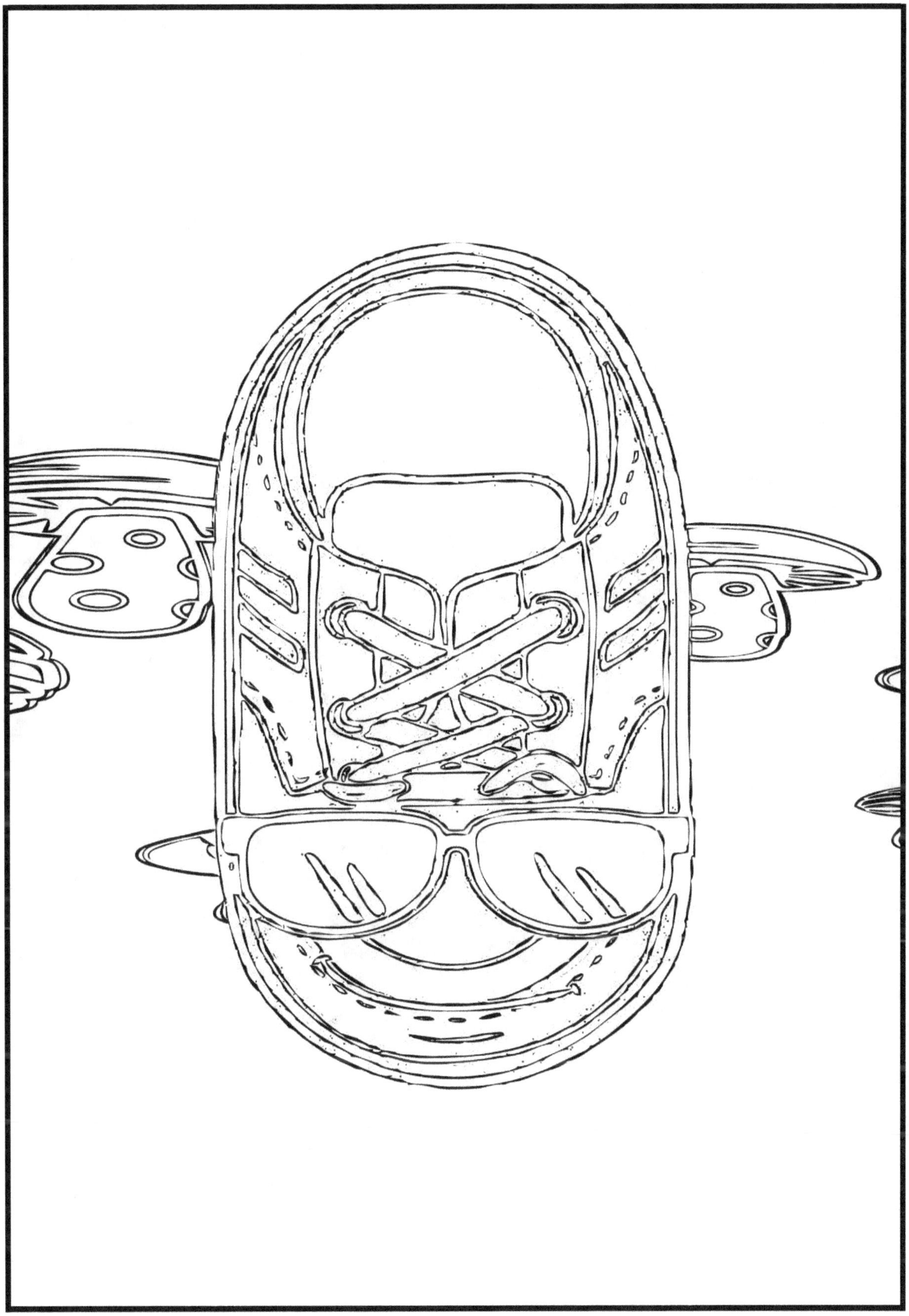

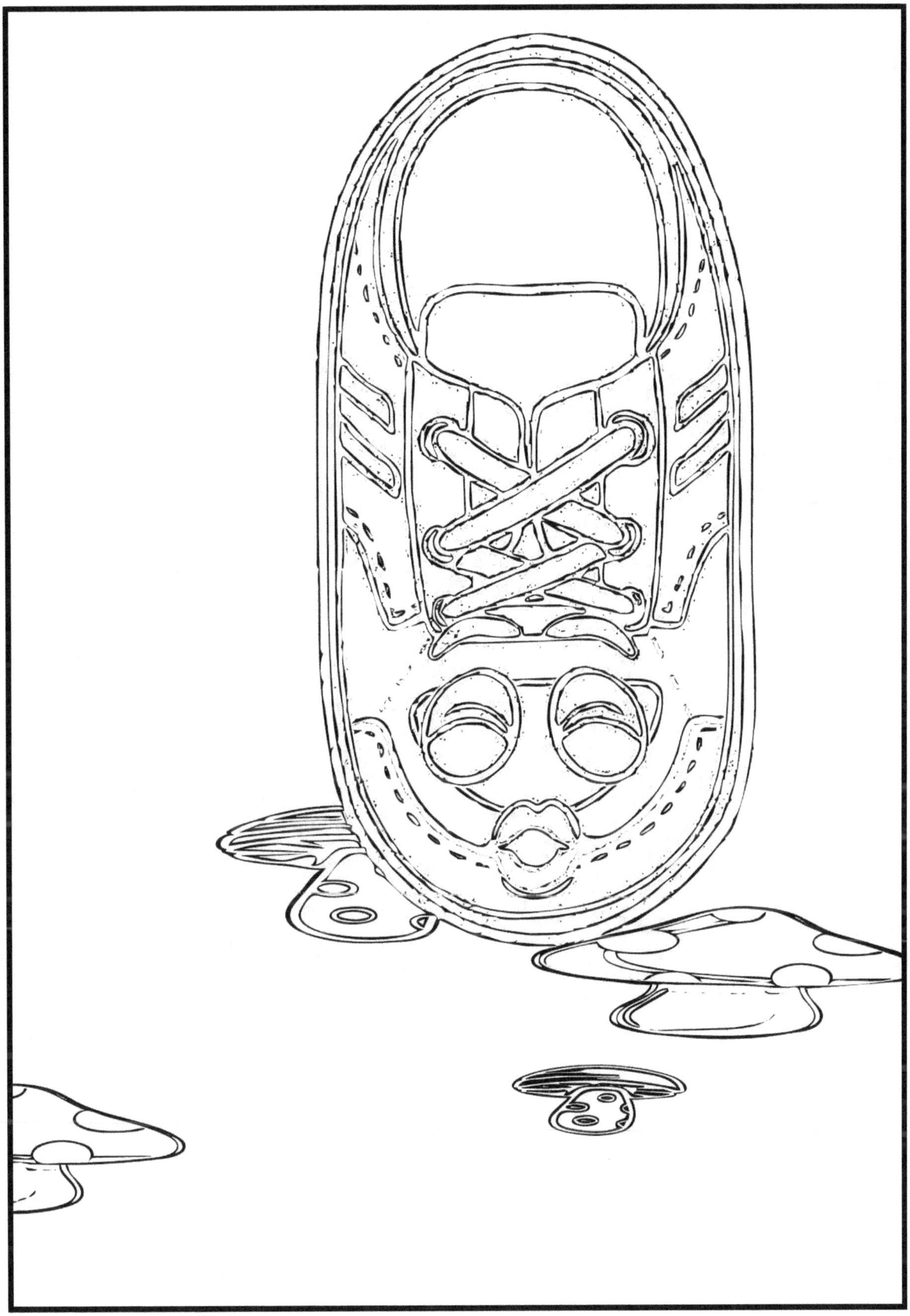

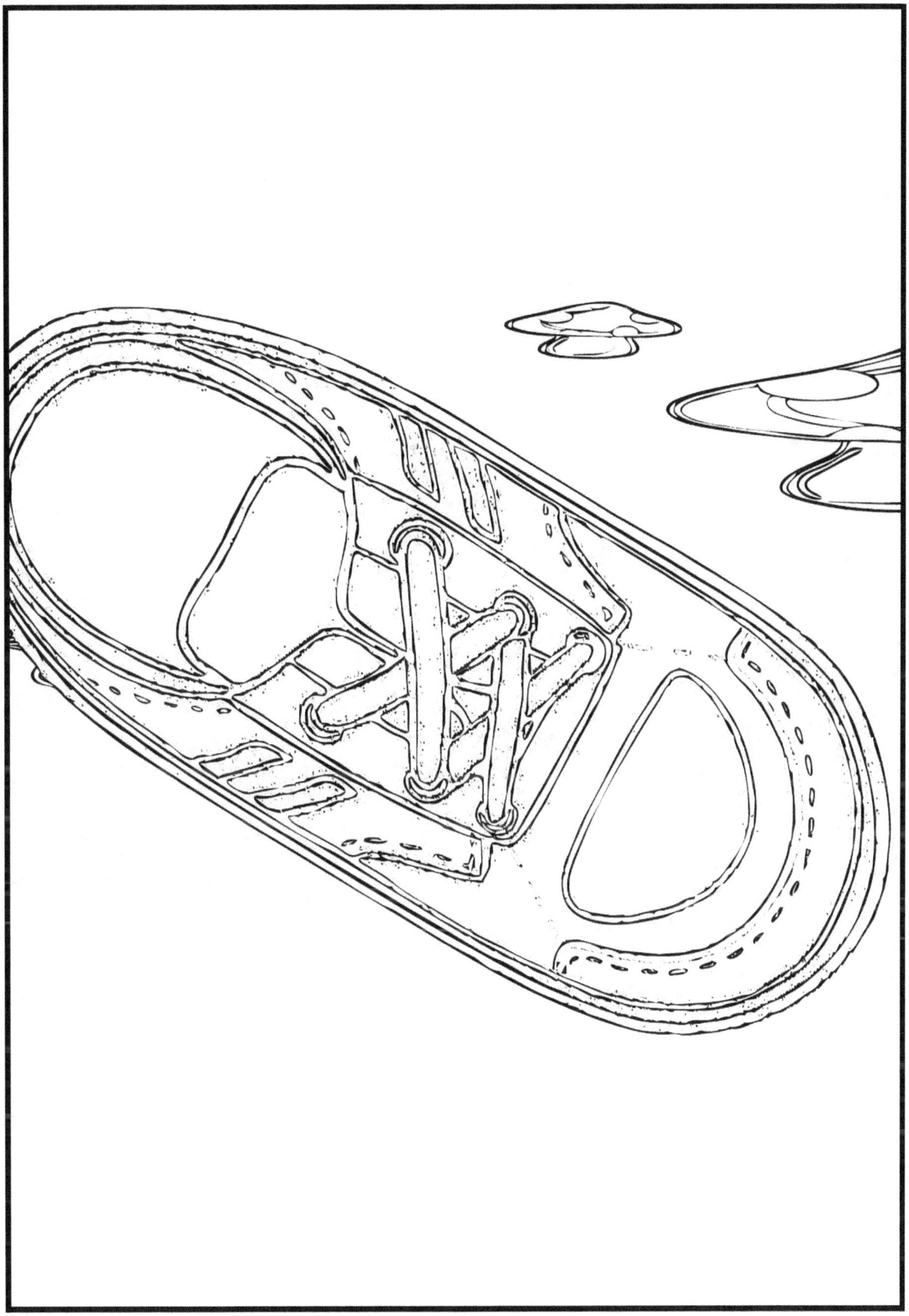

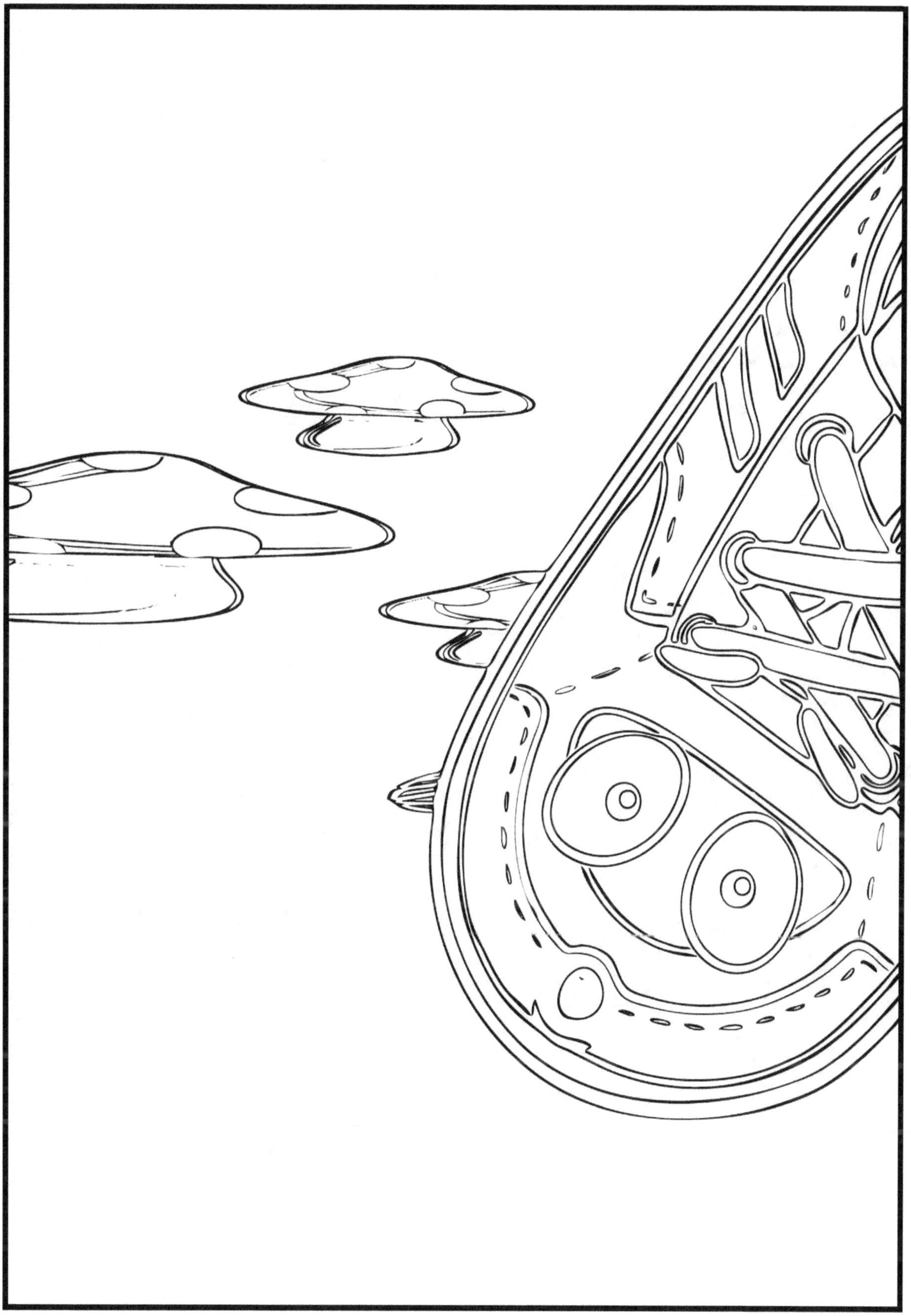

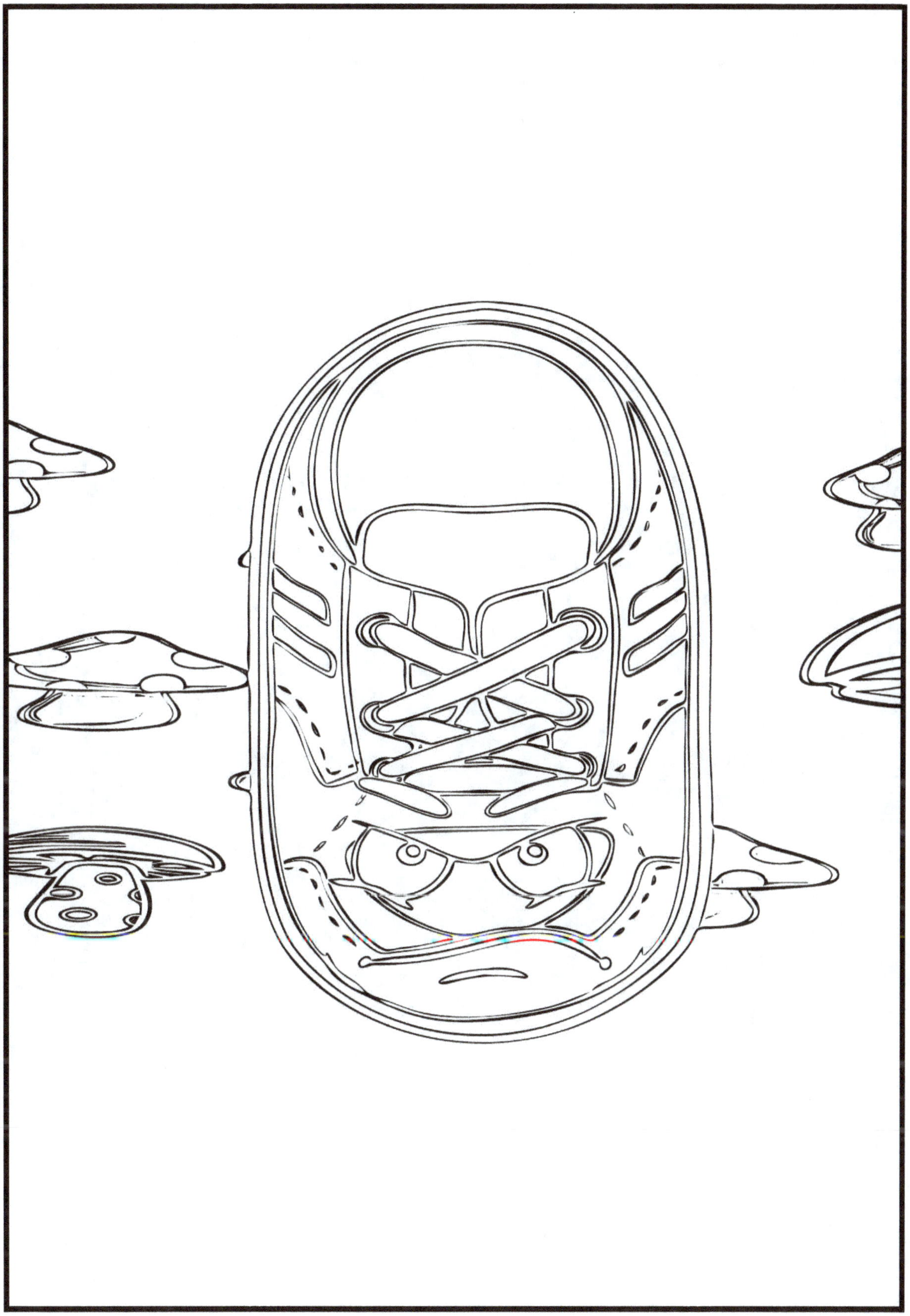

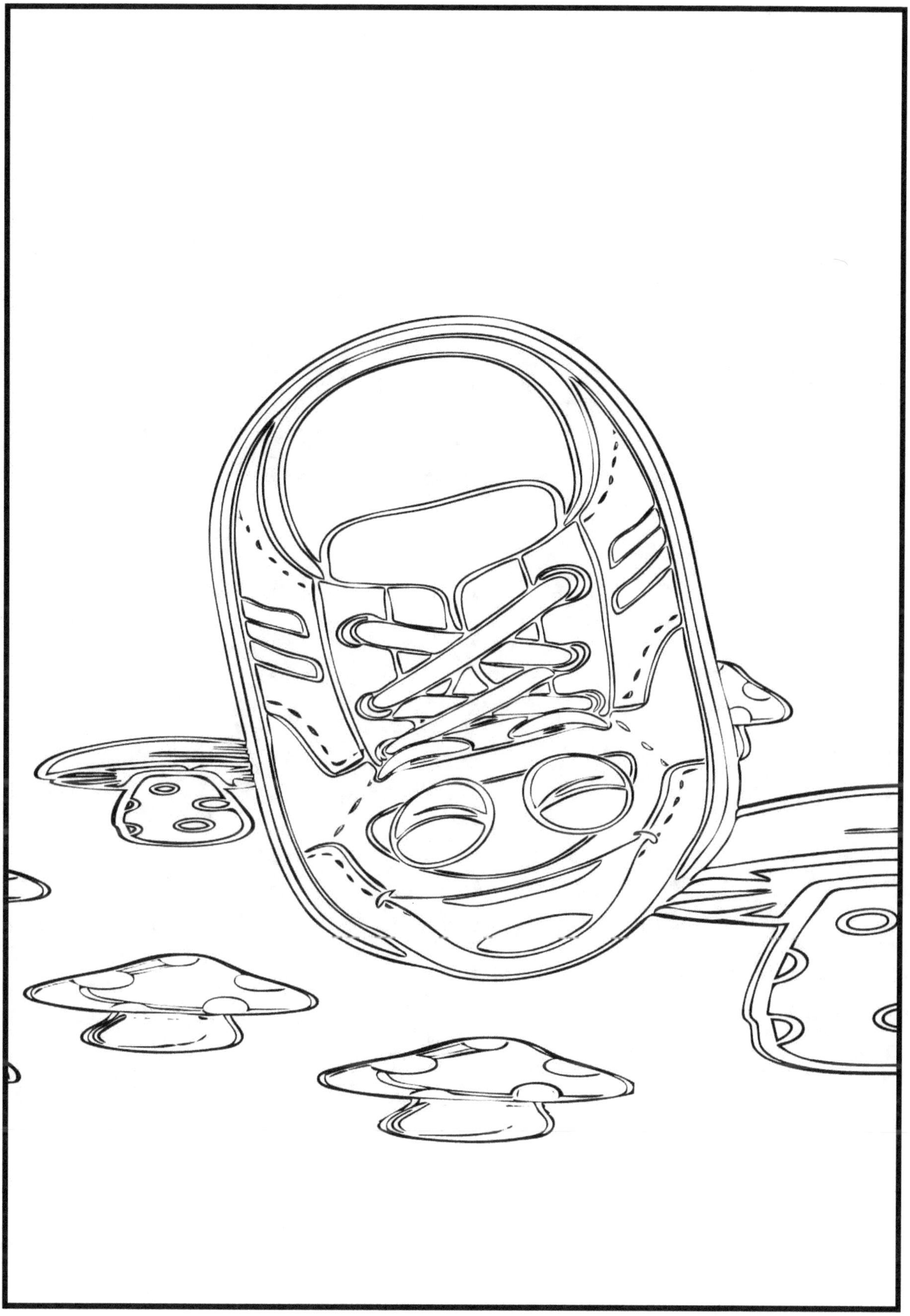

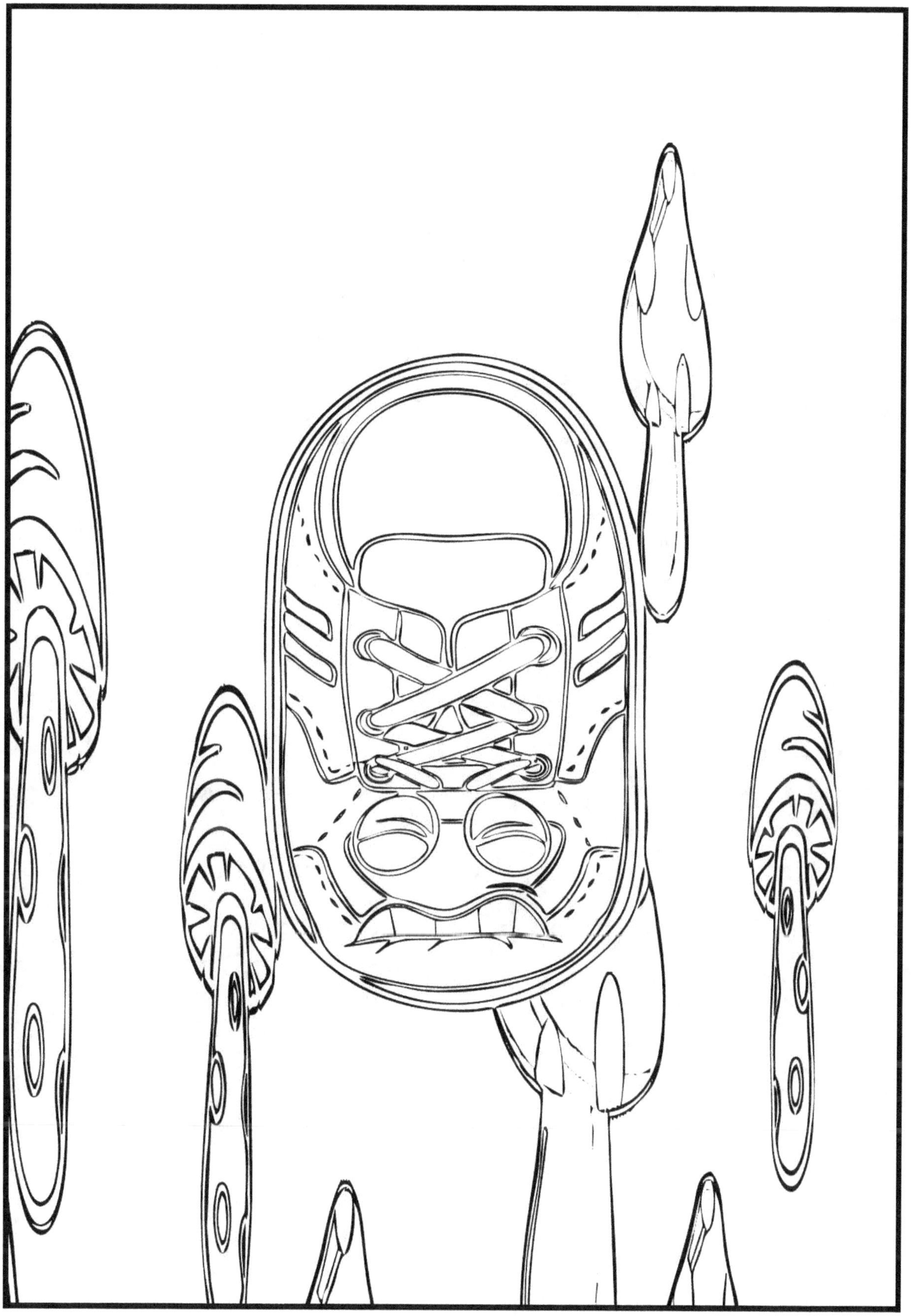

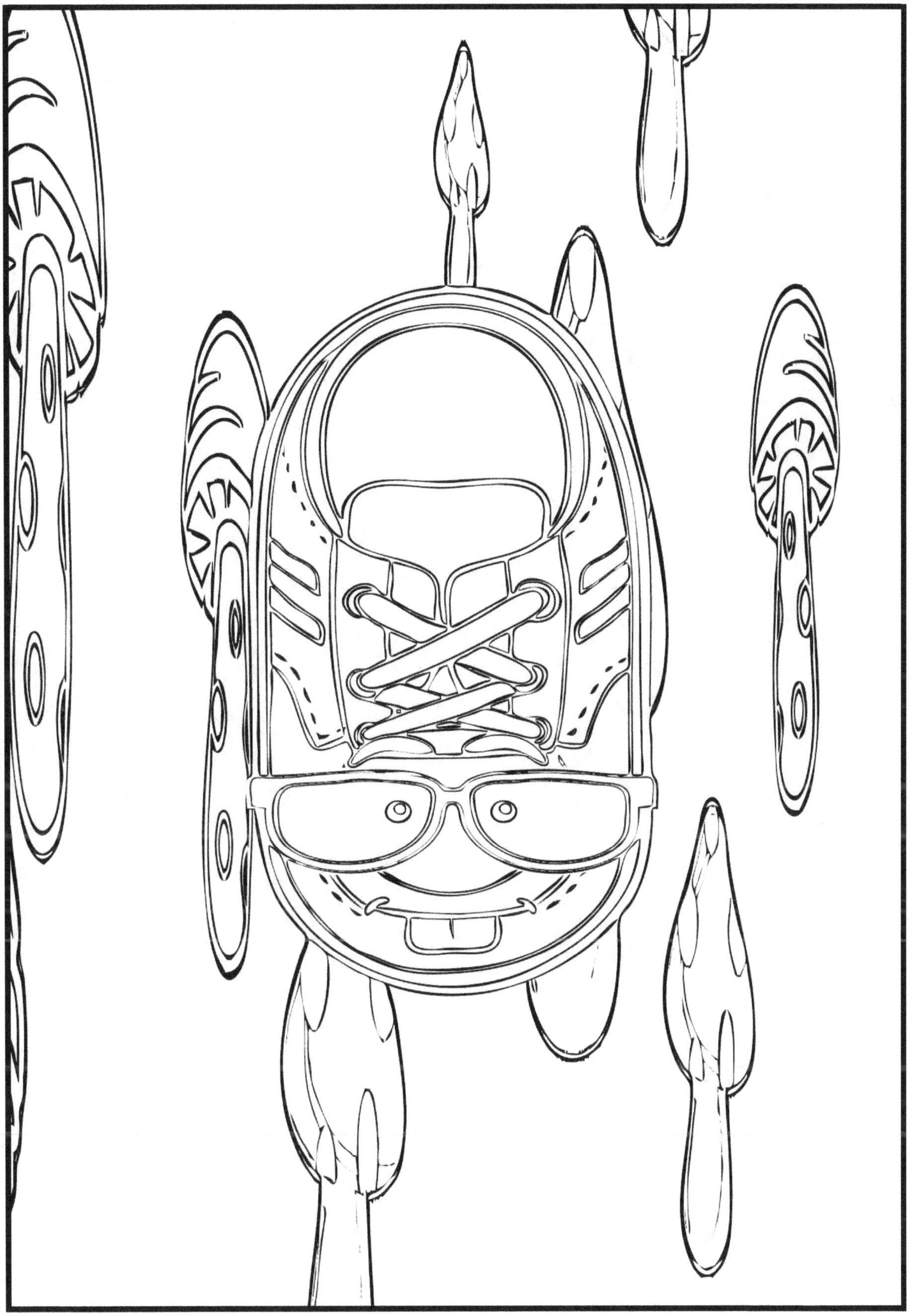

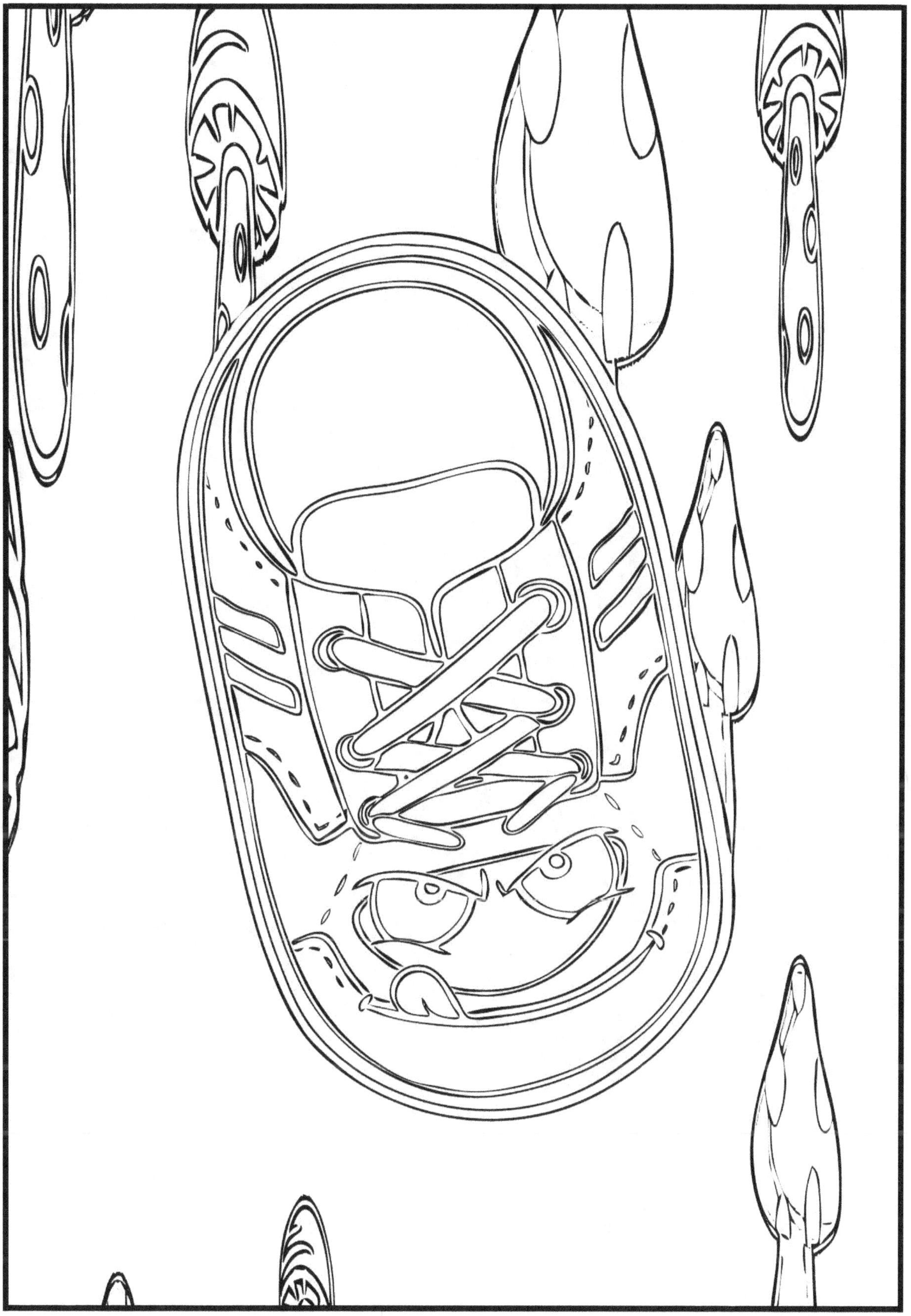

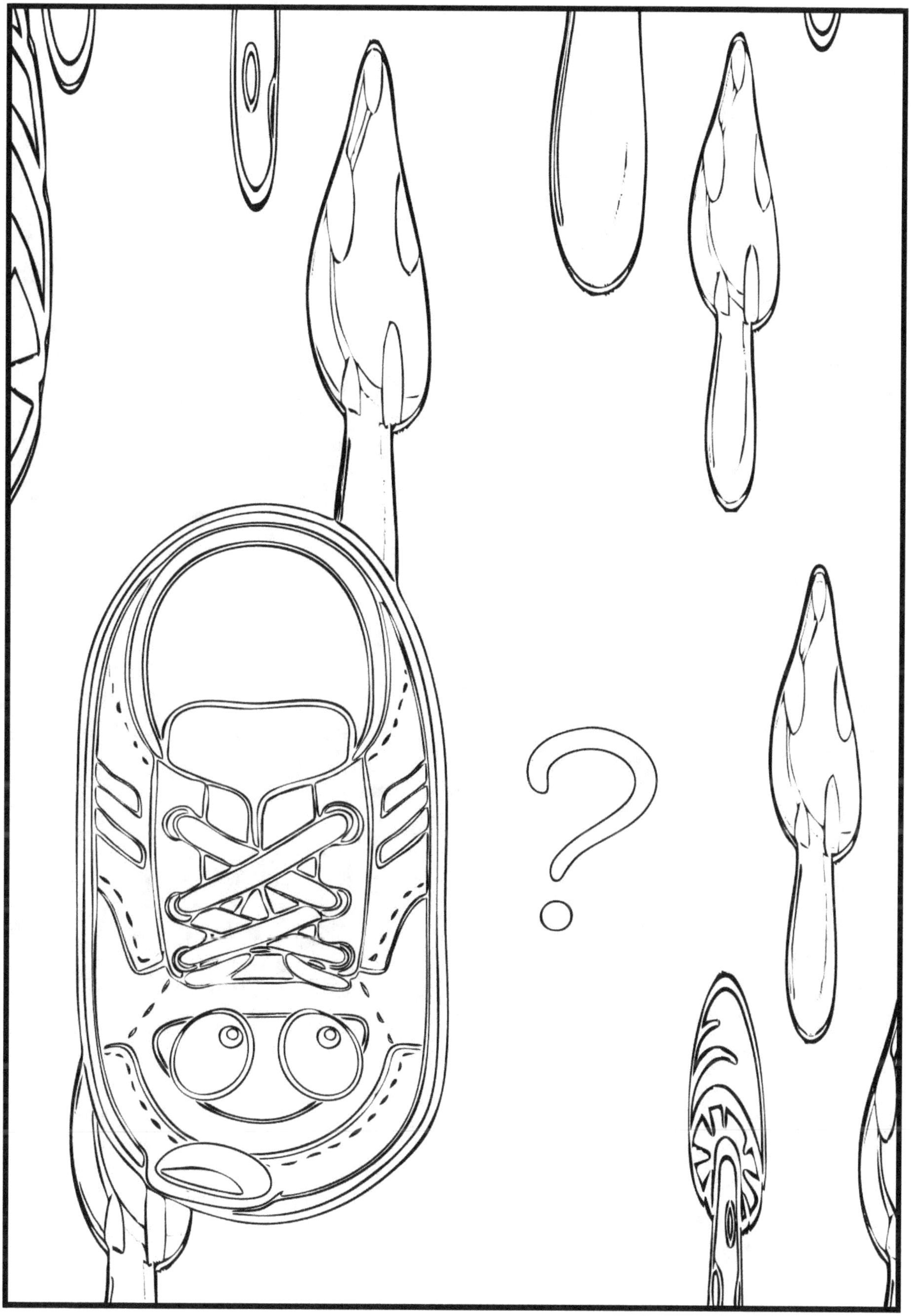

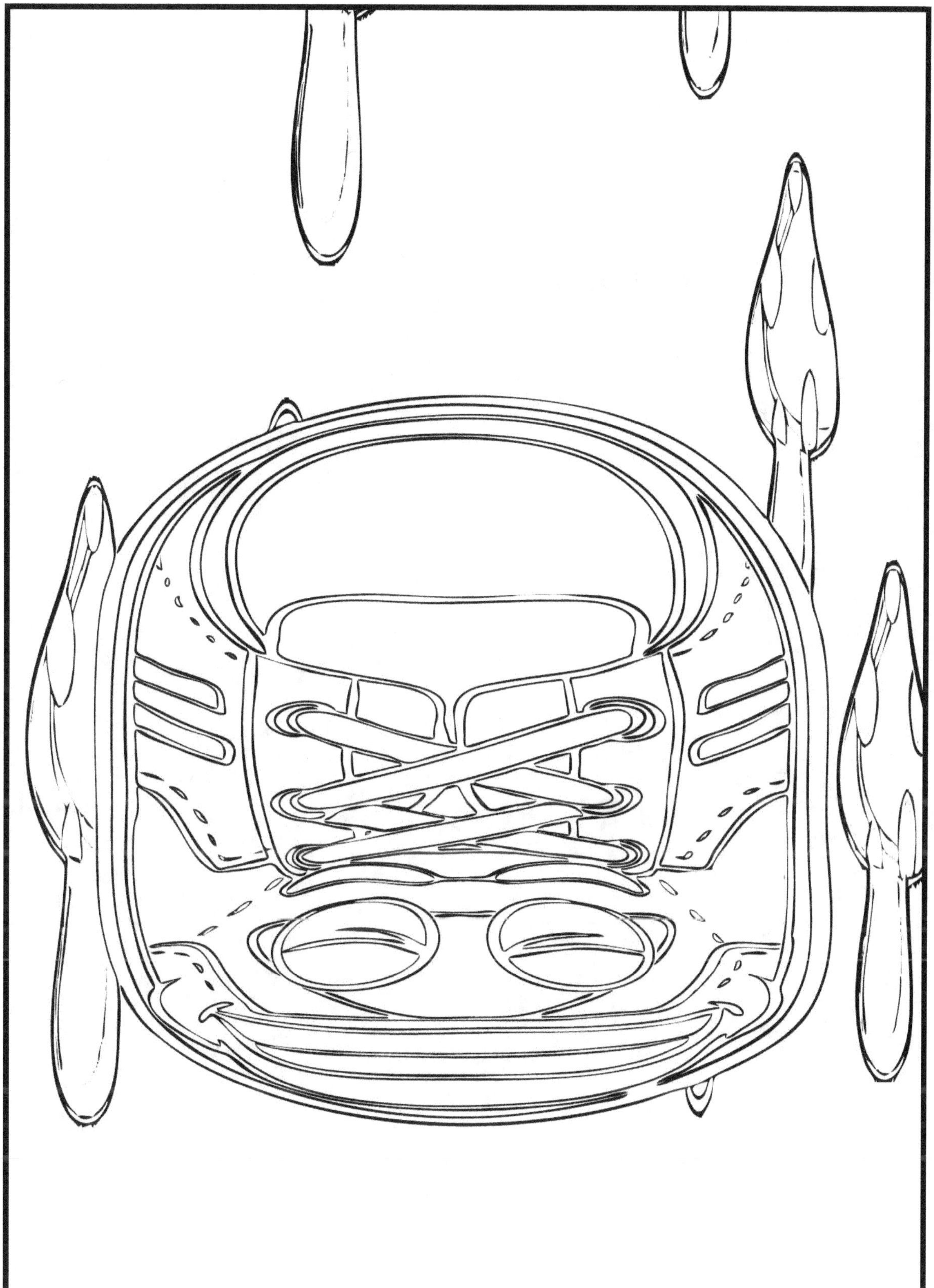

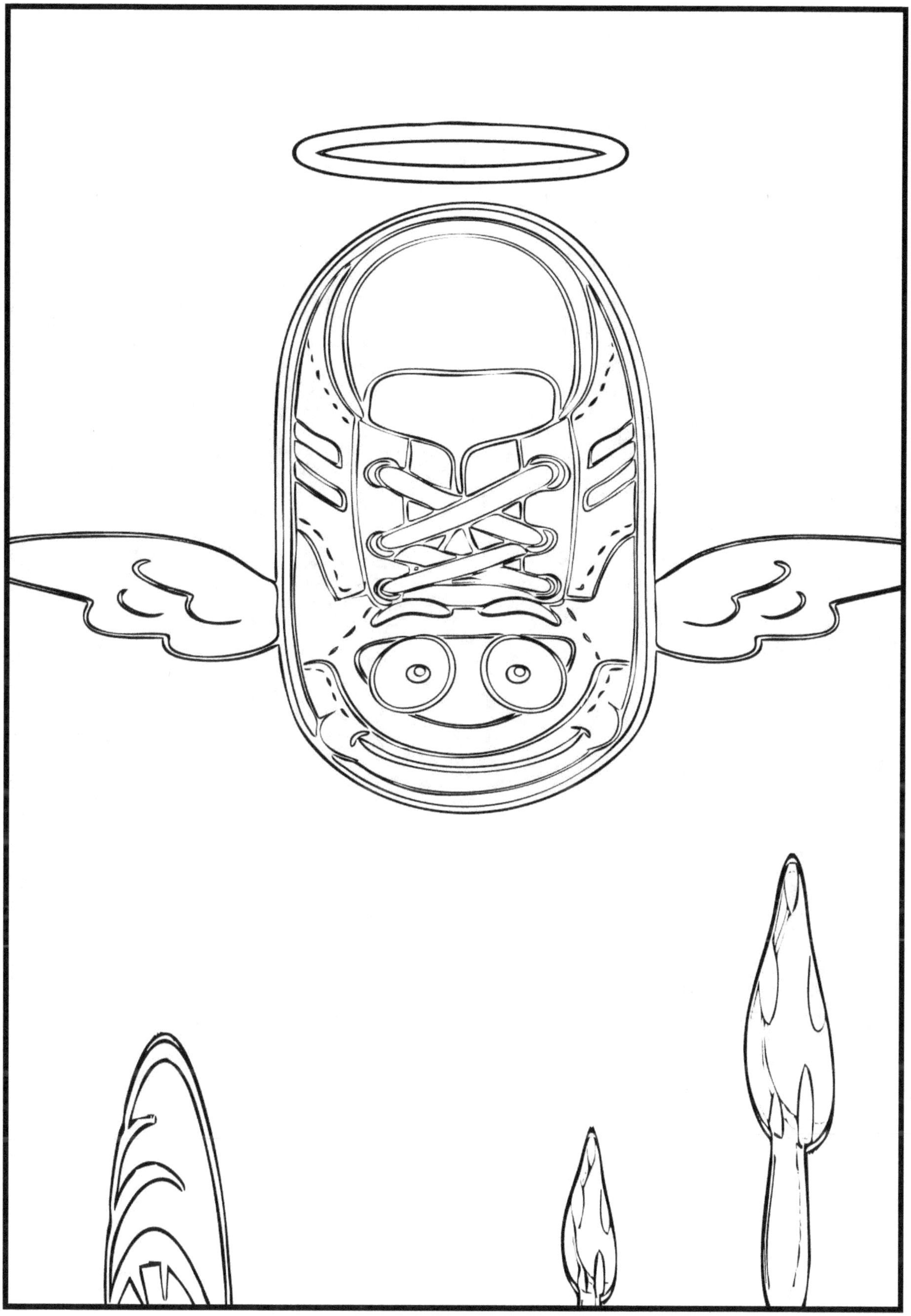

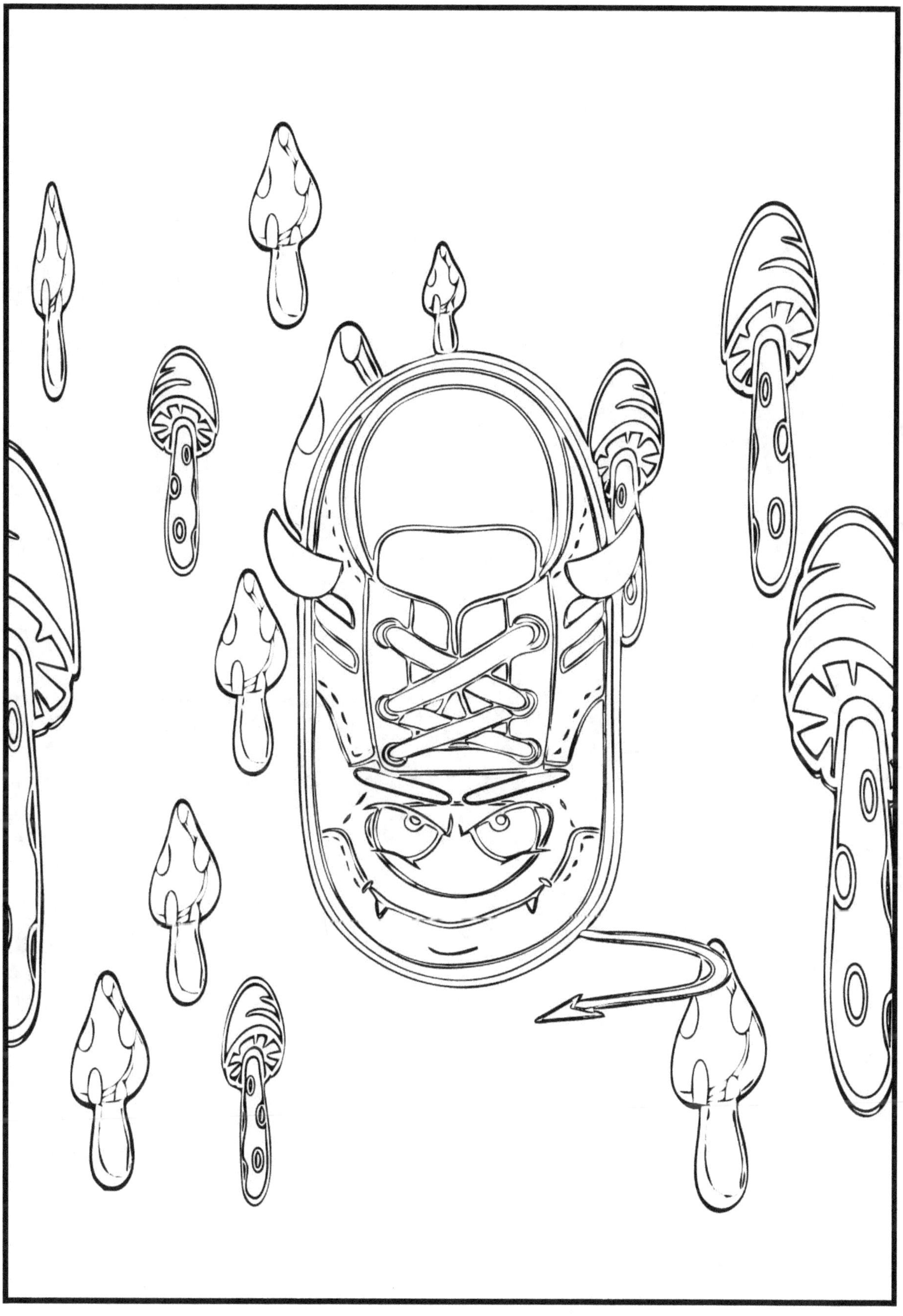

www.ingramcontent.com/pod-product-compliance
Lightning Source LLC
Chambersburg PA
CBHW081402170526
45166CB00010B/3171
* 9 7 8 1 5 1 9 6 1 5 9 2 3 *